keeper

Pitt Poetry Series

Ed Ochester, Editor

keeper

June 2014
Woodstock

for Bobbi~
sister poet ~
thank you so much
for being here !
With happiness in
meeting you~
Kasey

kasey jueds

UNIVERSITY OF PITTSBURGH PRESS

Published by the University of Pittsburgh Press, Pittsburgh, Pa., 15260
Copyright © 2013, Kasey Jueds
All rights reserved
Manufactured in the United States of America
Printed on acid-free paper
10 9 8 7 6 5 4 3 2 1

ISBN 13: 978-0-8229-6256-4
ISBN 10: 0-8229-6256-X

In memory of my father
And for

FFJ
VHJ
DPR
HGS

~family

Contents

keeper

The Bat

First dark, then more dark
smoothed down over it.

First sleep, then eyes
open to the ceiling
where something circles. For a moment,
you can't name it. And for a moment

you're not afraid. Remember

Blake's angels, how they leaned
toward each other, and balanced
by touching only the tips of their wings?
Between their bodies, a space

like the one just after rain begins, when rain
isn't rain, but the smell
of dust lifted, something silent and clean.

To Swim

Dear water, I loved you best
back then—my upside-down
house, kinder than sidewalks
or too-high branches, the bent red bike
that tipped me to the street.
Blue more blue and the quiet
more quiet, where I could be
the anhingas I'd seen, floating and diving,
there & gone & there,
swift as fists or Sunday school angels
parting the clouds of heaven.
I learned because my mother was afraid,
knew canals and pools, the eager sea
as so many places a child
could drown. I learned
because she loved me, and I fell
like Alice into somewhere else,
my feet leaving tiles or a motorboat's side
to ride on almost nothing. Because she was
afraid I called myself
a bird, a fish, and because
she loved me I tried
to be a boat, and grew myself
to fear and love until they
became like children, mine, twins
who looked so much alike
I could hardly tell them apart
or ever hold them close enough.

Two Owls

One an outline: simplest
shape, same dark
as the barn roof, and the horizon
I wanted to walk toward
and not stop.

Much later, the second, among
trees. A quickness,
wordless at first,
from the corner of my eye,
as everything huge arrives
without a name; then
the easy noises I called back,
a child's lexicon: big, brown,
strong. Almost

not there, gone so fast, wings
outside and in—the shocked velvet
of woods pulled over my head
like the blanket you spread
across me, our first weekend
away from school and drunk.
I fell into the haze of wine
like falling from the barn's peaked hill
of hay, that itch I'd carry
all day beneath my clothes—
straw-slivers and the welter
of stars where nettles
slapped my calves. A child's

lexicon: love, I, you.
Under knitted squares, the feather and hush
of different skin, I slept until you spoke
and woke me. Almost not there, gone
so fast: your voice, my first face.

Race Track, Hialeah, FL

I slipped my arms into a dress of fog
and the whole unbroken summer
opened to let me in: those mornings
my mother drove back streets
so we could see them: before heat
and crowds and bets
when clouds leaned close
but didn't speak, we leaned
on railings to watch the horses practice,
orbiting the track's green center,
its far-off oval of flamingos & palms
like the place on paper
where, years later, I'd set
my compass tip, careful
to make my circles *concentric*,
meaning they shared a heart.
Horses' hearts are huge,
their legs impossibly skinny.
At home I traced their shapes
from books, pressed so hard
my pencil left a moat around each photo,
a hollow that held them safe.
I trusted tile roofs and Banyan roots
dropping from each branch,
like the rope of the tire swing
that left me dizzy, spinning
between dirt and sky. All around, my city
spiraled out, coils of clay

widening a bowl to hold
the impossible things I was learning
to believe—how roots
could grow in air, or two lines
reach endlessly
and never touch. Even after
the horses left for other tracks,
swaying in the dark of trucks
with the highway's white line
licking always ahead, ticking
like August under my skin,
I curled in my swing, looped
my pencil around withers, pastern,
hooves, I leaned back
until my hair swept ground,
until the ground was sky,
asking roots and leaves,
our house, the horses, asking
all of it to remember me.

Skin

Five sharks in the scummed tank, clustered by a pipe
that pulsed clean water from the bay—

while the giant mechanical shark
caught in his cage outside the gates

turned and turned
above the highway that unraveled to the Atlantic.

They miss the ocean, my friend said,
cool steel of the aquarium fence

pressing our bellies as we leaned to watch,
their tails, their gills ticking patient

as the metronome over her piano, fragile box
that coaxed her notes to music. My friend

said even the skin of a shark
could cut you: under its silver

a million tiny blades. It was years before I'd touch
your skin and feel how terrifying

to swim that close to need—sharks' mouths
skimming the mouth of the pipe, and the mechanical shark

circling, never lifted
from the pole that held him, spellbound,

beside the highway, the unbearable
sea. I understood then everything

was real: shark, shark, metal and flesh,
skin that was not mine, the skin

that was, and how quickly blood
could stray from safe channels,

like snakes from a charmer's basket lured
into unforgiving air. How hungry

they must have been for each other, ocean
and shark, how cool and still

piano keys under anyone's hands
until the pressure, and then

music, your mouth
on mine, and one touch to lift

blood past its surface, that border
dissolved. How does it feel

to touch a shark? The fence
split my body in two: reaching,

rooted in bristling grass—
and across a hundred dusky streets

my house, my avocado tree, all the skin
I'd touch and touch—I would *want* that—

though I didn't know then, I still
don't, if any of it would be enough.

Copper

Summer dusks I placed pennies on the tracks
　　　　　and waited in bed
　　　　　　　　　　　to hear the night
　　　　train's whistle, waited
　　　　　　　for light so I could run
and lift them: flattened,
　　　　　　　　　strange,
　　　　　　　　　　　　　worn by weight
　　　　　　to a faceless shine.
　　　　One road in that town
and it ended in woods, maple and pine pressed close
　　　　　　　to keep their secrets
　　　　　　　　　　　safe, tossing them up
　　　　　　only once or twice
in the blue bathing suit
　　　　abandoned by the path, in snakeskin. Think skin

you can see through, soft metal, think a lake
　　　　　　　　　　so cold
　　　　　that from the boat your trailing hands
　　　　　　　turn pure bone.

　　　When someone I loved gave me pennies
he'd found, lifted for luck
　　　　from sidewalks and floors, I hid them in pockets
　　　　　　　and they glowed
　　　　where I could not see, rubbed together
　　　　　　　　　　　　like grapes in a vat
　　　　where they ferment, sluice of skin
　　　　　　　and juice into wine. For years

I wished on anything I could find:
        pennies tossed into ponds and pools,
    blood from a cut finger
                        tasting of copper.
I held snakeskin, sloughed-off
        skin of the birch tree
    white in woods; I heard the night train,
        felt walls shudder: something shakes
                the rooms inside, something
    moves the blood
                        that lifts the hand, throws the coin
    to make the wish, as grapes
lose their skins in the dark
        and in the dark the pennies wait,
            dazzled, dazed,
        utterly changed
            by the train I never saw.

Consolation

after de Chirico's The Enigma of a Day

Maybe he meant the distant town
as consolation, or the train's brief scribble of smoke.
The building in the foreground has so many doors,
but only one green-shuttered window,
too high to touch. The white flag rippled by wind:
high up, too—and below it the fierce edges
of smokestack and rooftop, the ineluctable light.
Even the statue turns his face away
from the two figures at the center,
and you can tell by their shadows
they are not touching: far-off and small.
Maybe he meant even their smallness
as consolation. The way you were small
that first time driving through desert,
the size of yourself measured against mountains
and not found wanting.
The sky's thin binding and the deliberate stars,
and you beginning that slow lesson—
how to be comforted by all of it,
by everything you could not touch.

Girl, 9, Secretly Snips a Lock of Another Student's Hair

She sees its color is like shouting, like singing
in church when all the notes
shoot skyward. And layered, like a lake,
dusky underneath where sun won't go,
where her toes might touch bottom or float
apart from her, vanish
into fish, lily, dark. This girl
is not her friend, but her hair
could be, it is so much, generous as pears
in a backyard garden before sparrows
pock and scar them, scatter their gutted husks . . .
        and it's her hand
reaching now for one wisp, such a smallness
that could, with luck, help her step
into some elsewhere—
like letters ghosting the sides of city buildings,
when just the *wing* of *sewing* starts machines
whirring in her head: she knows
it only takes a little, and it's her hand reaching
the scissors from inside her desk—she sees it
far off, shimmering, but it's her hand and not
like dying—what she knows
from books, squashed squirrels,
her grandmother's whittling down—but more
like waking on a snow day, her feet warm
where they rub together near the bed's end,
out her window the parked cars' edges
softened, swallowed, and even

in its highest branches where she
can never go, the thin oak holding what's fallen
up to the blank sky
that gives permission, makes possible.

Girl with Pigeons

Greek grave relief, 450–440 B.C.E.

She is saying goodbye
not to parents or sisters, not
to a servant or a friend.
Holding the pigeons, one in each hand,
she raises her arm to bring this bird's sharp beak
to her lips. Deliberate, her eyes open
to the precise meeting of mouth
and mouth, girl and bird, there where the stone
is unbroken and they are made
from one piece.

Girl in the Backseat, Wisconsin Winter

Between towns she studies the habits of dusk,
how bright things turn brighter
just before it's dark, and farm lights
stutter on. Mailbox, stop sign: she counts them without sound,

the backs of her parents' heads ahead of her
and dusking, too. She knows to keep
the window shut, her hands inside, remembers
her mother's warning: how her hands

could be hurt if they reached out,
if they fluttered open
in that blackness but they don't.
In between lights she holds her breath, thinking

if she breathes just right, in time with them, she'll own
these fields, snow-struck, winter-polished, her skin
scratchy with cold and on its way to somewhere
else. Her breath's a solid thing

but she knows she's liquid still, slipped like melt from icicles
on the phone poles that pin the road in place, steady
in the headlights, the shivering-down
night—so steady, now, she's breathing

with them, too, one quick inhale each time
they pass, the voices they carry flooding the wires, she could hear them
if she tried, if she stretched into this dark that's different
from sleep, hollowed as birds' bones,

that emptiness at the center that lets them fly.

Entering the Bath
after Bonnard

By the time she [Maria Boursin] met Bonnard on a Paris
street in 1893, she had left home, moved to Paris, found a job
and changed her name to Marthe de Méligny. . . . Not even
Bonnard learnt her real name until their marriage in 1925,
nearly thirty years after they began living together.
        Sarah Whitfield, "Fragments of an Identical World"

Her face is not visible,
not here. Here,
she is simply glimmer and skin,
naked, released
even from the green slippers she wears
in a different painting.
It is 1932. For years,
she's kept even from Bonnard
her real name, as now she keeps her head bent,
her face in shadow. Here, she is neither
name nor face but balance
on one bare foot, press of hip
into enamel chill. Here,
her whole skin glints,
a fish's river-bottom shine,
her lit breasts, her shoulders and knees
pink and brown and blue,
the orange curtain and purple tile
absorbed in her, reflected and cast back,
the room's ordinary objects,
clock and washcloth, bottle and brush,
sliding together, losing their edges,

letting their own names go.
Here, she is nearly
the fish she imagines,
glittering scale, magical lung,
stippled every color
in this late light. She waits
as water rises in the tub—
patient, released
from her green slippers, she waits
for evening to arrive,
for the painting to be finished,
for the bath to be full.

Stratus clouds form

when a layer of air is cooled
to the saturation point, and today
I want to call it kindness:
like lilacs permitting us their scent
just sometimes, off to one side
of the entire, rain-shined bush,
mountains keep to themselves
behind gray, thinking we can't hold
all of this at once. In Siena
I saw a leafless tree, covered
in oranges, and St. Catherine's head
preserved behind glass in the church,
as if too much wholeness
could be too much. Then last winter I forgot
about daffodils, and felt so surprised
when they returned, yellow all the way through
like a ball of wool that, even behind
a closet door, contains the baby's blanket
wholly in its globe, and waits
for our hands to begin.

Mackerel Sky

Under the morning's usual noise, the quarrels
of creek and trucks, a saw
insists its way through bark, taking down
the poplar. Circles inside the circle
of its trunk, like ripples a coin makes,
face up, face down,
falling. Seems we can only look
a little at a time, tenderness
has to surprise me, as the sheep did,
driven sudden from their barn, seamless confusion
of eyes & hooves & wool.
They looked frightened, but maybe
that was me, not knowing,
and the scaly clouds so close—
        which is to say I want to learn
to love you better, in this drift
of sawdust so fine and light
that, though the season's wrong,
for a moment I think it's snow.

Lost Things

I pass him at the bottom of the hill,
where the dirt road skirts two mown fields
then smooths into highway:
the dead raccoon,
curled close to the bank
with its blown gauze of Queen Anne's lace,
his face pressed between the precise stars
of his paws. Through my car window
he's one quick word swallowed into air.

It's not uncommon here
where oak and pine lick right up to the road's edge.
I've seen squirrels, a coyote, too many deer to count—
and, last week, a black hound dog
sprawled near a wire fence.
My eyes caught his red collar, the limp ribbon of his tail,
before he blurred in my rearview,
became any one of a hundred lost things—
a piece of tire, a child's tattered coat.

Now, at the stop sign, the road looks so clear,
a simple rope tying town to town.
I'm thinking how I love to drive:
the shift and shine of headlights,
how quickly a car will take you
anywhere new. I bump out onto the highway
and keep going, past the gas station, the tidy church,
more of those white flowers

that look like plates of stars, tiny blooms
just beginning to darken
at the edges, though I can't see that
from where I am now.

Translation

Finally the one small word
changed so many times
was simply left out
making space
for anyone to slip inside.

Butterflies at Santa Cruz

I couldn't see them
at first. Only eucalyptus
opening under blue fingers
of rain. Across our long
silence, your chilled hand
startled mine, showed me
where they slept, suspended
between leaves, rocked
in the wind's arms.
Some days everything else
looks like love. Wings curve
like a hundred clasped hands,
and night settles
over the ocean, one hungry
star at a time.

No Letters

After you've left, I walk
the dune's green shoulder, too far
from waves to see the empty suitcases
sand dollars have abandoned.
The sky, sad as old paintings,
holds your airplane somewhere
in its blue mouth, and all the letters
I will not write
line up in their soft coats
of ink. If I had a boat,
it would only float over words
the ocean hides, and touch
the water's long shine
with its wooden tongue.

Mission District, San Francisco

First invisible, then
everywhere: wild parrots
clattering from the alley, once
somebody's pets.
How did it happen, how
did their one room
turn to rooftops, bougainvillea,
the unsteady opera of the cars?
A girl in a taxi pressed her hand
to its window, fingers spread, a starfish
against aquarium glass. My first day here
I couldn't believe the palm trees.
There's a singing I knew nothing about.

His Letter

He didn't want to remember Ireland,
my mother says: her grandfather

in the South Dakota mines, writing home,
happy to have so much work. She smooths his letter

so I can see. Paper thumbed to almost-transparent,
cursive careful as a child's. And nothing

about Ireland. He didn't want to remember
the country I only know from postcards—

fishing villages, ponies in fields, any stranger's
easy images. What forges sadness so insistent

he needed all those miles to keep it at bay?
My mother folds the letter, slips it away,

back into the drawer where it's lived
for years, back into the dark:

paper meager and needed as a lamp
in the pit's extravagant black.

Sassafras

Held between pages of a book
itself held between others on the shelf:
a scrap of paper
with the lost friend's handwriting
in black ink. Because of the dark
inside, the words have not faded
as otherwise they might. The book,
unopened for years, opens
to this place precisely, without hesitation,
and without hesitation your body
knows the letters' shape, leaning gently
like thin trees in wind. Three words,
released by the press of darkness—
like sassafras, with its three
mismatched shapes of leaf:
oblong, mitten, ghost.

The Gift

All winter the feral cat
hid beneath the barn. Only sometimes
when I walked the rutted road,
kicking mud chunked in frozen fists,
she'd run ahead, always just on the edge
of vision. The woods stepped forward
in thin light, branches clean
as X-ray bones, the leaves,
by that time, vanished.

The cat, too: darted past,
slipped under the barn floor. Gone.
Mornings she left birds on the back porch,
dropped just by the door, and I tried
not to look too close, buried them behind the flower bed,
the one soft place I knew. That road stayed frozen
for months, trench and hollow dredged by trucks
then stiffened into place, lines my boots traced
all the way up to the birch wood and back.

I never thought to call them gifts,
the birds. Mornings I found bone-chill
air, husks of wing and blood, I tried not to look
too close, wanting October back again—
amber, amber, crimson, gold—not
the absent cat, the cold, everything
sliding past zero. The cat spread the feathers
in lavish arcs, and her eyes, as I passed the barn, glowed.
She left the birds for me. I'd spent months

staring at stripped trees, looking the wrong way
that whole time. It took a long time
to find what I needed: not the reaching
branches, but the ground.

December Underneath

I am not waiting. Here in the quiet
before faith or desire, two hands
settled me into the dark. Soil smoothed,
tamped down over my papery layers,
my thicket of just-begun roots.
To lie in mud and sift of leaves: eyeless
bed, shut-down space of worm and dirt
and stone: I have been chosen
for this. And I am not waiting
like winter, like snow forgetting everything
but her own plain dress. Forget me
in the hardened garden
under the weight of white.
I am not holding my breath. I am not
holding anything. Down where
nothing moves, there is no need for grasping
or the useless orange of the sun. A woman
who has forgotten speech
must learn the words again
slowly. Knowing each
as new. Sleep, daffodil, rain.
Let her be dumb and blind until then,
until one word fits her tongue
like a solid thing in the hand.
A bulb, or stone, before
it is cast back to the earth.

Foxgloves

The book says *Digitalis*, from the Latin
for thimble; says medicine

to soothe the arrhythmic heart. Says
tintinnabulum, meaning blooms

like bells, pendant in rows
over a church's stone

door. Inside each flower: balm,
though the book says too much

is toxic. How long before their luck
turns poison? What if you love someone

and never tell? Inside
that secret, a fern's spine, a stone, dark at the center

of the river. And foxgloves: one name for what guards
the finger from the needle, for bells and the silence

ringing harder when they ceased.

The Selkie Wife

Something else asks for her. She doesn't know
its name. Nights she lies down
in her body's longing; mornings, mends nets
for the man who hides her sealskin
out of love. Almost without her, her hands
continue to re-knot his ropes, making whole
what each day the sea separates
and frays, widening the gaps, the open spaces
through which it loves to pour.

The Missing Women

The ones on flyers pinned outside
the pool, papers curling in the chlorinated damp

where I'd wait, after practice,
for my mother, wait to be driven

away. The ones I'd study
over and over—names and faces and *last seen*

wearing, the places they'd disappeared
from. Days my mother came late I couldn't

stop staring, as if by looking hard
their stories would unlock: blue shirt,

bus stop, 1972: I carried them home
then back to the pool, up and down

my narrow lane, the water clear all the way
to the bottom, the slap and reach

of arms and hands—something missing
in me, or something I missed,

as every fall I missed the first leaves
turning, so when I finally remembered

they'd already started letting go,
their vanishing tangling the air.

That season I swam until my fingers puckered,
my still-damp hair, in the parking lot after, stiffened

to clots of ice. I swam and swam and my body
stayed solid, not like the water I knew

it contained. In school we learned how much
of us is liquid, how stories have

a beginning, middle, and an end. I read
of women who turned

to seals in the sea, dove deeper than I could
and came back safe, and I kicked,

turned, pushed away
from the wall, counting laps while the women

knocked inside my head, their weight
buoying me, acolyte of cold,

of split times, lane lines, the secret
history of water. How anyone could slip

from her story like that!—a shape
in paper cut cleanly away. Behind

my shape water sealed
itself shut, somehow I was swimming

into the next day, the next,
into love that seemed sometimes

a desire to be gone, whittled to the thinnest
stem of bone—as those women

might have desired, or not
desired, the ones so lost

by now they must be almost home.

The Selkie from Shore

You will tell me what I long for is God.
But I say it is bees, their pulse and tremble
in flowers slackening toward summer's end,
daylilies spreading rust under dusky oaks.
I say I want a garden for them,
so what is small might return
and be sufficient again. Not God, or sky
streaming light, cathedrals, a wish
I am not big enough to hold—not those
but the slightest tremor of air, and a humming
that has no need of me.

Wild Blackberries

Not sweet, not
tender: tasteless, almost,
save the first faint
acid sting, faint scratches
the canes leave, catching skin: seams
where the body opened
briefly, tangled
at the edge of woods where
every dark begins, deer track
between thorns too narrow
to follow, berries
weighing next to
nothing in the hand.

Robe

You slip it on while, elsewhere,
a painter removes
one object, then another
from each successive sketch.
First: arms through sleeves,
then the belt knotted close.
As first she subtracts the dog beside
the kitchen's open door. Then plates
laid carefully on the table,
the man seated nearby. Trees
outside the window, one by one.
Until only the necessary remains
in the room made itself
by absence. Its cuffs
brush your wrists' tender
skin, the hem lifts
in the slightest shift of air.

Fair Isle

Turn the sweater inside-out to show
the side called wrong: knots and lumps,

loose strands of wool tangle like weeds
in a ditch, late winter, lacings of stems

impossibly looped until, staring, you start
to see how it's made, how one

thinned branch, thornless, twines
the next and holds. Knitting, you carry

the unused yarn invisibly behind, brown then
brown then green, you keep weaving

one under the next, building the thicket that traps
heat near the heart, you try not to pull too tight.

Secondhand Dress

Somewhere between
blue and silver
color that asks
nothing in return
that returns
nothing you know
not river not window not swallows'
tilting flight
if you could remember
every evening pressed
beneath its silk
scratch of cuff against
whose wrist's inner skin
or how it slept or stayed
wakeful, floor-crumpled
in what room's
evenhanded dark
if you could
ask the question
say the one word
you have wanted to say
without speaking
even the faded
blur across the bodice
even the ripped sleeve
a keyhole
press your face
against the torn place
and the flowers
embroidered
around it

Window and Field

To be made
of absence
like this: outside
the painted window
rain falls hard
on a field—window
without the bars
it would have had
in life—and because
they are not, you
may enter
the field and walk
between stripes of rain
with nothing
to stop you or show
for it but
the damp briefly
darkening your hair
and the shoulders
of your coat.

The Sleeping Gypsy

after Rousseau

The painting shows no other sleepers, no sign
of road or town. There must be wind—
what else would blow the lion's mane
forward against his tipped-up ears?—
but nothing ruffles the man's rosy scarf,
his robe of colored stripes.
Above the curved half-moons of his closed eyes,
the real moon gleams,
its unreadable expression
meant to bless. The lion's eye
is open, golden, his nose
almost touching the sleeper's cheek.

Let him be touched.
Let him sense breath, wind,
another, wilder body's tide.
Moonlight on the mandolin beside him
makes each string shine.
His feet crossed at the ankles,
his mouth a little open,
here where no one lives
and everything sees.

Claim

Once during that year
when all I wanted
was to be anything other
than what I was,
the dog took my wrist
in her jaws. Not to hurt
or startle, but the way
a wolf might, closing her mouth
over the leg of another
from her pack. Claiming me
like anything else: the round luck
of her supper dish or the bliss
of rabbits, their infinite
grassy cities. Her lips
and teeth circled
and pressed, tireless
pressure of the world
that pushes against you
to see if you're there,
and I could feel myself
inside myself again, muscle
to bone to the slippery
core where I knew
next to nothing
about love. She wrapped
my arm as a woman might wrap
her hand through the loop
of a leash—as if she
were the one holding me
at the edge of a busy street,
instructing me to stay.

Keeper

Today I'm back
in the city where I lived, wondering
what the city keeps, what
of all the muchness
I've called mine.
Skin cells sloughed off,
invisible, mixing
with exhaust and dust.
Hair for a bird's house, breath
that flung itself out
to calla lilies, bougainvillea,
and came back changed:
a different blue, believing.
Blood each month
and more sometimes, when
a knife slipped or I skidded
on shaken pavement, running
the hills I never owned.
Love that returned to me and love
that didn't, spiraling endlessly
somewhere else, and today
it hardly matters
that I don't know where.
Gone so long, I came back wanting
what I missed, each fine grain
that slid or shivered
away, but I can't have again
what's already given, with
or without my knowing.
Now I am spread

in pieces over these streets,
Guerrero and Dolores: warrior,
sad one, shiners
of my bones. Now
I'm telling lemon trees,
the constant plums, I'm
telling you: I lived here
when longing
was the purest thing
I knew, always reaching
for something without heft
or breath that still, I swear,
moves and breathes
in, around, between
each fog-bound house—
where everything is something
I tried to keep, and
couldn't, and can't,
and won't, and won't
stop trying,
with this same heart,
always failing, infinitely lucky
and dumb, and these hands
that keep on
shimmering, wanting
to hold it all.

Cave Painting, Font-de-Gaume

So long it seemed like force—
the female reindeer, painted red, on her knees
before the larger, darker male.
Their faces almost gone
though his huge curved horns remain.
Only looking hard in that darkness, only asking
makes their shapes finally clear,
in the hollow where his tongue—faint, fading—reaches
to lick her bent head. At last even stone
must reveal its tenderness, as the swell of the wall
becomes his belly, her hip.

Deep North

For three years, my friend kept the dead songbird
in her freezer, until the power quit: cold cave,
like the one at Lascaux, closed
to visitors now. In its perfect dark
the painted animals gleam, lucent as organs
harbored under skin, carried everywhere
but never seen. In the middle
of her night, my friend is
painting: chickadee, whose name repeats its song.
I'd like to lie down a while
in the body that's mine, that part of Basho's title
rendered as *interior*, or *deep north*.

Bottle Gentian

This August, understand
what never opens. You thought

you knew about blooming,
about ditches lavish

with daylilies. But these five
fused petals live

on refusal, clamped shut like a mailbox
hoarding its letters. Each year

the river shifts, the old spruce—tindery,
brittle—comes closer

to falling in. Still, there are days
you want it all, not knowing: the precise

line between woods and field, between
gold grass and pine-and-dimness—

and the way a hummingbird's shadow
flickers on the table,

how something so small could tremble the light.

A Kind of Vanishing

Through the words that are in me I tried to decipher the night,
and then remembered that darkness has its own resolution.
Kristin Prevallet, I, Afterlife

In total darkness, the eye
refuses to adjust. Think
of the mailbox, tin door shut
over letters—maybe
the one I hoped for most.
I imagined it inside: absolute
night, and the fierce glow
of that white envelope like some dusk-
opening flower, or ghost translucent
at the edge of woods. Just once

I'd find that kind of vanishing: abandoned
silver mine, Rhiolyte, Nevada. Where one bulb
gave way to candles, then
to this. I knew I could never
draw curtains so tight, or close
my eyes without the inner lids'
glimmer of red. How perfect the things
we are not meant to see. When I reached in
only newspaper, bills, and that blackness
rent and gone.

A Field Guide to North American Wildflowers

Each page holds a flower, each flower
a story: one named for the scarlet

of cardinals' robes; this next,
swallowed, a cure

for sorrow. Fleecy leaves
of mullein once lined shoes,

and its blossomed stem, dipped
in oil, made a taper

for those who could not sleep.
Blue vervain, butter-and-eggs:

names comfort on the days
you can't say what's gone.

Bluebird House

Build a wooden box and settle it
at the field's edge. To steady
the nails, place your hands

just so. Already it's night
inside the box, inside
the shadow of pines. As if

you could add those darknesses
to make more dark. Or hold

the intricate circle of twigs before winter,
when you remove the abandoned nest.

Rufous-Sided Towhee

I tried so hard to speak.
When the mountain laurel outside
fills with birds,
I will begin again.

This time not *sorrow*, but *sparrow*.
Not *gone* but *wren*.
Inside the bush, a fluttering, then

colors startle and sharpen: brown-gray
back, stain of rust
under wings—and a name

I didn't know I knew

blooms behind my eyes,
whole, unbroken.

In this way, maybe,
I will remember your face.
Not by trying, but by birds.

The Door

Early Netherlandish Painting at the Metropolitan Museum of Art

In these paintings of the Annunciation, the angel appears to Mary in a small walled garden, or what the guidebook describes as an "early bourgeois interior." Instead of a bare Bethlehem kitchen, rooms lit with drapery and silver; instead of rocky, dun-colored desert, the soft greens and blues of the artists' home.

And everything takes part in the heavenly visit—the whole Monday morning world breathing and moving in the ordinary, astonishing light. Two pink hollyhocks by the crumbling stone wall as much as the angel's iridescent wings; the horse's shining rump, the silver shoe visible on his upturned hoof as much as Mary's blue robe and patient hands.

In one painting, she has been reading—her Bible lies open to a page filigreed with flowers. In another, the window behind her frames a courtyard in which two men stroll, discussing cattle or the weather.

Most show Mary's eyes fixed on the angel, but in this one, she gazes outward, toward her watchers, so calmly—as if there were no distance between those lilies and wings and this museum room, as if we could all enter that place so easily, as simply as stepping through a door.

A Fragment of Sappho

The words I love stand by themselves.

The way I'd stand
before a door not yet open.

Waiting.
Almost whole.

I long and seek after—
nothing more. Not wind itself

but how a tree bows down
to be swept clean of leaves.

A real door,
painted white. The other words are lost.

Secondhand Sweater

Serpentine of stitches
twisted left to
right: the cabled pattern's
not simply beautiful but
deliberate, a thickness
meant to warm
the wearer, to bind heat
against the heart
each pattern unique
so drowned fishermen
made unknown by
weeks or months
of water might
be known again
through crossed and coiled
ropes of yarn climbing
the body, intricate as
a princess's braid
let down from
a tower window
water undoes
the body but not
the complicated plait
of wool will last
I swim my arms
through its sleeves

The Selkie Returns to the Sea

I used to think my longing had an end.
I dreamed the sea so many years, the sea
became a dream. Now I search its swells
for anything to pin me down.
Fishing boat, buoy, whip of kelp; even waves
that vanish too fast, leave silence
in the spaces between. On land

my kitchen harbored smallness: sweet
oat cakes, my children's silky heads. When I
return to them next spring, on the flood tide's
seventh day, I'll touch my mouth
to the house's wall, a baby learning the world
with her tongue—stone and
salt, the garden leaning into bloom,
my sealskin just another dying I've put on.

Cusp

Between highway lanes the median blooms, late
late summer thicketed with weeds. Between coming
and going, a little hitch, a seam—
Snow White in the kitchen, forgetting apple and wedding,
meadow rue stitched to her apron's hem.
Behind her, windows hold the forest
so gently, for once its trees don't recede
or beckon, but stop as if listening
to something they can't quite hear.

Wood

I pressed the side of my head to the table
and heard your voice vibrate
the grains of pine—as if love
needed a medium, some common substance
to travel through. Even the splinter:
you held my foot in both hands
to free the shard of redwood
tunneling toward bone. The foot, accustomed
to carpet and pavement, the dim interior
of shoes: it felt a little shy, turned up
to air, the sterilized tweezers and needle; a little glad
for the world that works its way in
in spite, or because, of the sting, the throb,
the humming that rides the looped highway of blood
up from that glimmer of pain, sadness shifting
like the thinning of fog, in which the edge
of one tree comes clear.

It moves

like a kingfisher skimming the river,
like hummingbirds that blur and dart.
Minutely, as even fixed stars
move, their travel traced by years of patient eyes.

Like clouds, or like a coin in water, slow-falling
toward other bright or tarnished hopes.
Like flame chewing a match, a bicycle's
spoked wheels. Like pollen. Pressure. Snow.

Or like roses sent as a gift,
inside a box inside a truck
inside the night. Or the woman
who waits for them, reading in bed,

who doesn't know
she's waiting; who probably doesn't think
of petals just then, of what
in any dark space might appear.

The Fire Road

Some pinecones need flame
to open. Only heat

cracks loose their tongues, lets the tree
seed itself, repeat green syllables

across one field and the next.
In woods along the fire road

this morning: branch, vine,
tangle of your hair, vein of leaf

and hand. Saplings strung
between boulders and stumps—no telling

which will live. I planted
two roses, side by side

in equal light, but by summer
only one. . . . And that lost wallet:

how my dumb hands
dredged my bag, lifting

aspirin bottle, keys, everything
but what I needed. So often

it's easier not to talk or touch,
not to see pigeons rising

from the barn roof, all one body
in a shout of wings. But then we bake gingerbread

together, and what my body
can't do without:

cinnamon, vanilla and honey, heat
opening the cells, the tongues

of pity and plenty. It enters
every crack, every thirsty

blinded space: whatever it is
makes pigeons lift together, awkward

and sure, makes salmon press upriver,
milkweed spill its inside silk,

saying *nobody loves you, nobody*
loves you like I do.

The Underpainting

X-radiographs demonstrate that Vermeer initially included a dog in the doorway and a gentleman in the back room [in A Woman Asleep]. *The artist, however, painted out these figures, leaving the viewer alone with the woman.*

Arthur K. Wheelock Jr., Vermeer: The Complete Works

Because the words
will never be right

now that everything is written
for you, I erase

and erase the page,
again, again

rub and sweep
until even blankness

might begin
to dissolve,

the paper's milk-
and-sugared sturdiness

worn through
to the blue behind

and between
clouds' ceaseless pull, the place

where man and dog, painted over
by Vermeer, linger

in the hall beyond
the maid's closed eyes.

She leans above
her wineglass, the dog's paws

shudder into sleep,
and the man opens

his mouth,
hesitates,

then begins to speak.

Notes

"To Swim" is for my mother.

"Translation" refers to three versions of Master Dogen: "the body exposed to the golden wind," "the body exposed in the golden wind," and "the body exposed, the golden wind"—and is for Ryushin Sensei.

"The Missing Women" includes the title of Silvia Curbelo's book *The Secret History of Water* (Tampa, FL: Anhinga Press, 1997).

"Fair Isle" is for Grace Shin.

"Window and Field": The painting is Van Gogh's *La Pluie*.

"Deep North" is for Sarah Masters.

"A Fragment of Sappho" quotes from Anne Carson's book of translations *If Not, Winter* (New York: Knopf, 2003).

"Wood" is for Andrea Szeto.

Acknowledgments

Much gratitude to the editors of the following publications, in which these poems first appeared, sometimes in earlier incarnations:

Barrow Street: "Lost Things"; *Beloit Poetry Journal*: "The Bat"; *BigCity Lit*: "Claim"; *Crab Orchard Review*: "Entering the Bath"; *Faultline*: "Butterflies at Santa Cruz"; *5 AM*: "Bottle Gentian," "Foxgloves," "Girl in the Backseat, Wisconsin Winter," "It moves," "Wild Blackberries," and "Wood"; *Global City Review*: "Rufous-Sided Towhee"; *Hawaii Pacific Review*: "No Letters"; *Lumina*: "Girl with Pigeons"; *Manhattan Review*: "The Missing Women," "Girl, 9, Secretly Snips a Lock of Another Student's Hair," and "Sassafras"; *Many Mountains Moving*: "The Gift"; *Marlboro Review*: "The Fire Road" and "Two Owls"; *Poet Lore*: "Consolation"; *Prairie Schooner*: "Cave Painting, Font-de-Gaume"; *Puerto del Sol*: "Skin"; *Runes*: "Mackerel Sky" and "The Selkie Returns to the Sea"; *Salamander*: "Race Track, Hialeah, FL," "To Swim," "The Underpainting," and "Window and Field"; *Southern Poetry Review*: "A Field Guide to North American Wildflowers" (as "Guidebook").

"His Letter" appeared in *American Diaspora* (University of Iowa Press), edited by Virgil Suarez and Ryan G. Van Cleave.

"Cave Painting, Font-de-Gaume" has been reproduced from *Prairie Schooner* 79, no. 1 (Spring 2005) by permission of the University of Nebraska Press. Copyright 2005 by the University of Nebraska Press.

"Bottle Gentian" was featured on *Verse Daily*'s website (www.versedaily .com).

The epigraph for "A Kind of Vanishing" is from Kristin Prevallet's *I, Afterlife* and is used with permission by Essay Press.

The italicized text in "A Fragment of Sappho" is from *If Not, Winter* by Anne Carson, copyright © 2002 by Anne Carson. Used by permission of Alfred A. Knopf, a division of Random House.

I am beyond lucky to have the following people and places in my life. Thank you, thank you to: Alan Boudreau, Wendy Taylor Carlisle, Carla Drysdale, ETS, Suzanne Gardinier, Jennifer Giordano, Hogen Green, Peter Greer, Liz Hecht, Laurie Miller Hornik, Minter Krotzer, Joan Larkin, Patricia Lee Lewis, Valerie Linet, Thomas Lux, Emily Mieras, Linda Pastan, Naomi Shihab Nye, Doug Rogers, Pat Schneider, Elaine Sexton, Jill Silverstein, Hal Sirowitz, Andrea Szeto, Judy and Godfrey Tomanek, Jean Valentine, Coly Vulpiani, Anne Weiss, and Florence Wetzel, for everything they have taught me and showed me and helped me to be; Ryushin Sensei, Shugen Sensei, Hojin Osho, and the sangha at Zen Mountain Monastery, Mt. Tremper, NY, for keeping the ground under my feet; Soapstone, the Ucross Foundation, the Vermont Studio Center, and the Virginia Center for the Creative Arts, for sanctuary; the staff at the University of Pittsburgh Press, especially Margie Bachman, David Baumann, Lowell Britson, Joel W. Coggins, Kelley Johovic, Maria Sticco, and Alex Wolfe, for their kind and patient care of this book, and of me; Mary Bisbee-Beek, for embodying generosity always; Sarah Masters, for invaluable artistic friendship—and for the beautiful cover art; Julie Greenwood, for help with technology and beyond; Tarn Wilson, for so many years of yeses; Grace Shin, for making everything possible; Ed Ochester, for his amazing faith in these poems; my mother and sister, for their boundless love; Dennis Reil, for putting the heart in me every single day; and Linda Elkin: first teacher, best reader, darling friend.